I Am Free
Meditating on the Scriptures

By Linda Patarello

I Am Free
ISBN: 978-0-9896919-4-9

Copyright © 2013 by Linda Patarello

Editor: Daphne Parsekian

Published by Orion Productions, LLC.
P.O. Box 51194
Colorado Springs, CO 80949
Orionproductions.tv

These small books with scriptures that fit each theme are meant to help you learn how to meditate. Each scripture has my own meditative thoughts that follow, and my hope is that this will help you understand the thought flow that can happen when you think on God's Word. As you begin to think and ponder on God's Word for yourself, you will find more revelation in the Scriptures. The Holy Spirit will reveal it to you personally. I encourage you to read my initial book, How to Meditate on the Living Word; it will explain in more detail the process of meditation.

Your victory has been paid for by Jesus Christ, but we live in a world where there is evil. While you live here, every single day you need to hold your shield of faith up. We have an enemy who is out to destroy us, to lie to us, telling us we don't have the victory. The fight, then, is for your mind, so every single day you must live by faith, which means you don't let down your shield no matter what. You believe the word of truth and that He has already given us the victory. You and I must take the land and enforce that victory!

"Wherefore take unto you the whole armour of God, that ye may be able to withstand in the evil day, and having done all, to stand."

Ephesians 6:13

Amplified

"Stand your ground."

After you have put on the whole armor of God, you are to stand firmly in your place. When an army stands their ground, they hold their position and don't let the enemy through. For a Christian, you are called to stand on God's Word. We do not let go of God's Word; we choose what He says above all else. Just like a bull dog holds tight and doesn't let go, we are to hold on to the promises of God.

"Now the just shall live by faith."

Hebrews 10:38

We have been given five senses to help us in this world, but they were not meant to lead us or to take over in our lives. God is a God of faith and He lives by faith; He speaks of things that are not as though they were. We are His children, and we should live the same way. To live by faith means that faith is a priority in your life above feelings and above circumstances.

"And the devil that deceived them was cast into the lake of fire and brimstone, where the beast and the false prophet are, and shall be tormented day and night for ever and ever."

Revelation 20:10

Satan is the deceiver and the father of lies. He has brought destruction to millions of people; he has murdered children and anyone else who stood in his way. There is coming a day when God is going to cast the devil into the lake of fire, and he shall be tormented day and night forever and ever. He has already been defeated by Jesus but has not yet been captured to be thrown into the lake of fire. I believe many millions of believers will be mourning for the souls that did not choose Jesus, those that will be destined for hell. But those same millions of Christians will be cheering to see Satan thrown into the lake of fire where he belongs.

"For this purpose the Son of God was manifested, that he might destroy the works of the devil."

1 John 3:8

Jesus is God come in the flesh. Jesus, the Son of God, came in boldness to destroy all of the works of the devil. When He was on the earth, anywhere there was sickness and disease or demons wreaking havoc in people's lives He showed mercy by reaching out to heal and bring freedom. He had the authority. Satan is a thief (John 10:10) and comes to steal, kill, and destroy. This should be our same attitude wherever we are. We should hate evil and destruction and take our authority that has been given to us. We should not stand idly by and watch. When we have His Spirit living in us, we are equipped to break the bonds and heal the sick.

"And having spoiled principalities and powers, he made a shew of them openly, triumphing over them in it."

Colossians 2:15

Amplified

"[God] disarmed the principalities and powers that were ranged against us and made a bold display and public example of them, in triumphing over them in Him and in it [the cross]."

The Lord disarmed the principalities and powers. To disarm means to take the weapons away. Now they have no weapons, no power—only deceit. He not only disarmed them, but He made a spectacle of them, a bold display for all to see. Those in hell saw. The angels and the spirit realm must have seen. Perhaps those who had passed away were able to see. He didn't do this act in a shy way, but He triumphed instead. All the credit that we give the enemy is a shame. We let ourselves sometimes believe that he is stronger than God. What a lie that is.

"And ye shall know the truth, and the truth shall make you free."

John 8:32

There is truth, and there is the lie. Jesus is the truth, the way, and the life. Jesus brought the truth. He didn't come to condemn the world; He came to save it (John 3:17).

Once your eyes are opened to the truth and you see with your heart, the truth makes you free. To be free is a wonderful thing. Freedom comes from God. He has the power to make you free. He wants men free to know the truth. Bondage comes from Satan. Religion can cause bondage, but the Word of God can set us free.

"If the Son therefore shall make you free, ye shall be free indeed."

John 8:36

In Mark 5, we read about the man who dwelled among the tombs with an unclean spirit. Men would often bind him with chains to control him, but he would rip them off and no one could control him. He was being controlled, instead, by Satan and was in terrible bondage to him. The Bible says that always, night and day, he was in the mountains crying and cutting himself with stones. There was a legion of demons inside of him. He was trapped as if in prison. This is how he lived until Jesus came and commanded, "Come out of the man." After it was all said and done, the man was found sitting, clothed, and in his right mind. Only Jesus can do this for good. When Jesus makes you free, you are completely free for good. You will never be trapped again, unless you let it happen. His Word will keep you free.

"Being justified freely by his grace through the redemption that is in Christ Jesus:"

Romans 3:24

8

You could say justified means "Just as if I'd never sinned." How can this be? One would say, "Don't I have to earn this?" No. This is a gift. It is by the grace of God. You can never buy it. Your redemption has been paid for. A high price has been paid by the Son of God, Jesus Christ. It is yours for the taking. Just receive your redemption. You've been redeemed by the blood of the lamb. Through His sacrifice on the cross, your redemption is here today.

"But not as the offence, so also is the free gift. For if through the offence of one many be dead, much more the grace of God, and the gift by grace, which is by one man, Jesus Christ, hath abounded unto many."

Romans 5:15

The wages of sin is death. Adam sinned and brought death to all. We were then all born into the sin nature because of Adam. The wages of our sin is death, but the free gift of righteousness is different because it is not earned. It is given. You as a receiver don't do anything but receive when a gift is given to you. The one that gives the gift is responsible for choosing and purchasing it. It is by God's grace that righteousness is given; the offense of Adam abounded unto all, but His free gift has also been given unto all who will receive it.

"For he that is dead is freed from sin."

Romans 6:7

When Jesus died on the cross, He took all of our sins—past, present, and future—with Him. When He took our sins, He paid for us to have His life. And when we received Him, His Spirit came to live inside of us. Our old sin nature died on the cross with Jesus. Romans 8:10 says, "And if Christ be in you, the body is dead because of sin; but the Spirit is life because of righteousness." So if we are alive with Him, we have also died with Him. Our sins, our past, our grief and sorrows, and even our sicknesses and bondages are all gone. You could say it this way: Now that my sin nature has died with Jesus, I am freed from sin, I am freed from bondage, and I am freed from sickness.

"Being then made free from sin, ye became the servants of righteousness."

Romans 6:18

If I am free and the devil is defeated, then I can choose, with my free will, to serve God with my body, my will, my mind, and my emotions. No one has a noose around my neck any longer. No one is twisting my arm. I am free to choose life. I am free to choose the way I want to live from now on.

"But now being made free from sin, and become servants to God, ye have your fruit unto holiness, and the end everlasting life."

Romans 6:22

Our fruit used to be bent toward evil, but now we are freed from sin. We have become a servant of God and unto God. We now have new fruit unto holiness, and it will just keep getting better—a new life, a clean life—all the way into the forever with the Lord with life everlasting. Peace and freedom forever and ever. It is mine because I am loved by Jesus. I am loved by the Holy Spirit. I am greatly loved by my real heavenly Father (Matthew 23:9).

"For the law of the Spirit of life in Christ Jesus hath made me free from the law of sin and death."

Romans 8:2

Now that you are "in Christ," the law of the Spirit of life in Christ Jesus has made you free. You are not under the law of sin and death any longer. The law of sin and death brought guilt and condemnation. Being under the law is always having the mirror in front of you, where you are forced to see your mistakes, sins, and weaknesses. When Jesus died on the cross, He fulfilled the law. You are under a new law now that is full of God's life, peace, and freedom from bondage. Grace reigns. You have peace with God, and you are His own. You are accepted in the beloved. You are loved. When you know you are loved, you want to do right and please God. You live by leaning on His strength and not your own any longer. He supplies all that you need.

"He that spared not his own Son, but delivered him up for us all, how shall he not with him also freely give us all things?"

Romans 8:32

God the Father did not spare Jesus. He did not hold on to Him. He gave Him for us. God SO loved the world that He gave His only begotten Son. The true test of a real giver is when they are willing to part with something that is most valuable to them. There are times when God will ask us to give something that we have treasured for a long time. He'll say to us, "Give that to so and so." We'll say, "No, Lord, you don't mean that, do you?"

Once we surrender to this thought and obey, we will have peace; but, it's always a hard thing to do in the beginning. But it is good to obey and let go. When we do, we experience, in a tiny way, what God felt when He gave His most prized possession, His Son Jesus. When we give up something, we want to know that the one who receives it will take care of it. God delivered Him up to take the sins of the whole world, to carry all of our grief and sorrows, to be made sin and to take all of our diseases. The pain in God's heart to bear this must have been tremendous, but He was willing. If God freely gave His own Son, shall He not also freely give us ALL things? All the promises of God in Him are yes and amen (2 Corinthians 1:20).

"For whosoever shall call upon the name of the Lord shall be saved."

Romans 10:13

This is a very short and simple verse, and yet even from the simplest verses you can glean a lot of wisdom. Taking a few words at a time, we focus on the beginning "whosoever." This can be anyone, regardless of your ethnicity, your upbringing, or your religion; regardless of one's fame or fortune, political status, or royal standing. A child, or even a homeless person, can be a whosoever. As long as this whosoever can call upon the name of the Lord, they can be saved. It does not specify the place even. One need not be in any large cathedral to call upon the name of Jesus. Jesus is the one who saves, and we are the ones who call. Anywhere, anytime is good. "Shall be saved" is the outcome. They shall be saved from hell and eternal damnation, from darkness and bondage.

"Stand fast therefore in the liberty wherewith Christ has made us free, and be not entangled again with the yoke of bondage."

Galatians 5:1

If you were set free from a prison, would you want to go back again? We must hold on to our freedom. Every day we can choose life or death; that is up to us. He is telling us to stand fast and hold on to our liberty. Choose it every day! Stay there. He paid a heavy price to set us free; why would we want to go back? Don't get tangled again in that trap. Old things are passed away, and you are not a loser anymore. Get the right perspective. You are a child of God. You have been delivered from the power of darkness.

"Christ hath redeemed us from the curse of the law, being made a curse for us: for it is written, Cursed is every one that hangeth on a tree:"

Galatians 3:13

Deuteronomy 28 speaks about the curses, but Jesus became the curse for us. It is good, however, to read those so you can see what He took and what you have been redeemed from. In the Old Testament, if you were hung on the cross, you were cursed; it was common to have that done outside of the city gates. We were meant to go to hell, for we have all sinned and fallen short of the glory of God, but He did it for us.

"For as much as ye know that ye were not redeemed with corruptible things, as silver and gold..."

1 Peter 1:18

It wasn't silver or gold that saved us, but it was something much better and surer. If silver and gold are corruptible, that means they can be destroyed—they can and will be corrupted one day. We were redeemed by the blood of the lamb (Colossians 1:14). The blood of Jesus is holy and pure, perfect and spotless. His blood was the perfect offering, and it was incorruptible. This means our redemption is forever and will never end.

"And they sung a new song, saying, Thou art worthy to take the book, and to open the seals thereof: for thou wast slain, and hast redeemed us to God by thy blood out of every kindred, and tongue, and people, and nation;"

Revelation 5:9

It is the four beasts and twenty-four elders that sing a new song, and this verse then explains what the words of the song are. Picture this: Verse 8 states that they each have harps. They are gratefully singing a most beautiful heavenly song, with honor and reverence, "Thou art worthy to take the book, and to open the seals thereof: for thou wast slain, and hast redeemed us to God by thy blood out of every kindred, and tongue, and people, and nation…." Only He is worthy. Only He redeemed us. Every one of us has been paid for, if they would only come, believe, and receive what He has done.

"Let the redeemed of the LORD say so, whom he hath redeemed from the hand of the enemy;"

Psalm 107:2

We shouldn't hide it or be ashamed of it. We should speak it to ourselves and anyone who will listen. The hand of the enemy was too strong for us.

14

We couldn't save ourselves. He rescued us. Jesus is our champion.

"But now thus saith the LORD that created thee, O Jacob, and he that formed thee, O Israel, Fear not: for I have redeemed thee, I have called thee by thy name; thou art mine."

Isaiah 43:1

If you are in Christ, you are grafted into His family. He created us, and it is God who formed us. We should not fear, for it is He who has redeemed us. He made us, and He rescued us; He bought us back. He has called us by each name. He knows us. We belong to Him, but not in a taskmaster sort of way. Remember that God is love and everything He does comes through the motivation of love. When no one wanted us, He did. When we have suffered rejection, He won't ever reject us. When some have left us, He will never leave us. He loves you. He will always want you and is glad to call you His own.

"I have blotted out, as a thick cloud, thy transgressions, and, as a cloud, thy sins: return unto me; for I have redeemed thee."

Isaiah 44:22

Your wrongdoings and your rebellion used to be as a thick cloud. Imagine a thick black cloud in the sky, dark and shadowing the land, so threatening as it moves. With one wave of His hand, He wipes it away, and the sky is blue and clear again; the bright sun is shining and you again feel its warmth. He has erased your sins. He doesn't see them. He has cleared the way. He did it for you because you were unable to. And then He brings the invitation, "Return to me. For I have redeemed you." You see, He wants you. He is waiting for you to make the choice.

"Sing, O ye heavens; for the LORD hath done it: shout, ye lower parts of the earth: break forth into singing, ye mountains, O forest, and every tree therein: for the LORD hath redeemed Jacob, and glorified himself in Israel."

Isaiah 44:23

So poetic is the redemption of man. All the heavens are called to sing! The valleys and the mountains and all of creation are called to break forth into song! Every tree of the forest and every green tree of the whole earth come and shout, come and sing! God has glorified Himself; He has glorified love. He has redeemed Jacob. And we that are in Christ are also included in Jacob. He has redeemed us and purchased us back rightfully through his Son. All the wrath for sin was placed on Jesus. Now we can sing the song of freedom! There are songs from one's own country that declare emancipation. But they cannot touch this heavenly song of redemption!

"Therefore the redeemed of the LORD shall return, and come with singing unto Zion; and everlasting joy shall be upon their head: they shall obtain gladness and joy; and sorrow and mourning shall flee away."

Isaiah 51:11

We are the redeemed of the Lord. We should not be moping and depressed, downtrodden and dreary. We have a right to be full of joy. We are the ones who should be putting on the garment of praise and the laughter and shouts of freedom. We should let our light shine and cast off sorrow and crying. We are on the winning side, the victor's side. He has won. No more fear, no more running, only joy, only peace.

"The Spirit of the Lord God is upon me; because the LORD hath anointed me to preach good tidings unto the meek; he hath sent me to bind up the brokenhearted, to proclaim liberty to the captives, and the opening of the prison to them that are bound; To proclaim the acceptable year of the LORD, and the day of vengeance of our God; to comfort all that mourn; To appoint unto them that mourn in Zion, to give unto them beauty for ashes, the oil of joy for mourning, the garment of praise for the spirit of heaviness; that they might be called trees of righteousness, the planting of the LORD, that he might be glorified."

Isaiah 61:1–3

In Luke 4:21 Jesus spoke this passage and said, "This day is this scripture fulfilled in your ears." Jesus came to set us free. He came to preach the good news to us, to bind up the brokenhearted, to proclaim liberty to the captives. He came to do all these things for us. He came to heal our hearts but not only that. He also came to make us strong in Him that we might cast off that spirit of heaviness and put on the garment of praise. He has given us all that we need to be like Him, for He is in us. We have His Spirit. He's provided and given us His authority so that we, in turn, can go out and preach the gospel and set the captives free. He has passed the baton of life to us. All of these wondrous works glorify Him. He did great works, and greater works shall we do in His name because He has gone to the Father.

"David said moreover, The LORD that delivered me out of the paw of the lion, and out of the paw of the bear, he will deliver me out of the hand of this Philistine. And Saul said unto David, Go, and the LORD be with thee."

1 Samuel 17:37

Even in the physical we can look to our God to deliver and protect us. There are plenty of promises for that. We take them and stand on them. We believe and speak them fully expecting that He is real and protection is ours. David discovered this truth. For him to say that the Lord delivered him means that David was looking to the Lord to help him. He wasn't counting on his own strength. He knew that he was no match for the bear and the lion by himself. We can trust in God for all things. When we get rid of the pride and humble ourselves under His mighty hand, He will lift us up. He will deliver. The uncircumcised Philistine was no match for God. Keep your eyes on God and His mighty ability. If we look at the problem, it grows big in our eyes. If we look at God, we will see His greatness.

"He delivereth me from mine enemies: yea, thou lifteth me up above those that rise up against me: thou hast delivered me from the violent man."

Psalm 18:48

Your enemies are God's enemies. Satan is our enemy, and he hates anyone that God loves, but he was no match for God. God sent Jesus. He lifted us up out of hell. We, in all rights, were destined for hell. But God, in His grace and mercy, delivered us and brought us up with Him to sit in heavenly places in Christ Jesus. We have been made joint heirs with Christ (Romans 8:17).

"I sought the LORD, and he heard me, and delivered me from all my fears."

Psalm 34:4

When we seek the Lord and draw near to Him, He draws near to us. He has already pursued you. He hears His children. And if you want to receive Jesus as your Lord, He hears your call. All that call upon the name of the Lord shall be saved (Romans 10:13). He delivers you from ALL your fears. Not one shall stay in your heart. You can have complete confidence as you trust in Him and His word. You are in a new family now that loves, provides, and delivers.

"For great is thy mercy toward me: and thou hast delivered my soul from the lowest hell."

Psalm 86:13

He does not save us out of obligation. He doesn't bring it up later and remind you of all the trouble you caused. He loves you, and His mercy is great towards you. He wanted to come to your rescue. He couldn't wait to ransom you, to forever adopt and care for you as His very own. God gave His Son. Jesus was willing to go and die. He went to the lowest depths of hell for you in your place. By the power of the Holy Spirit, He was raised from hell and from the dead. You have been raised with Christ. He has delivered your soul.

"He sent his word and healed them, and delivered them from their destructions."

Psalm 107:20

The word that He sent was Jesus, and Jesus healed us. That is His nature: to help, to heal, and to save. He is the one who delivered. You may have noticed that this is all past tense. He sent, he healed, and he delivered. Jesus delivered us from our destructions. We were on our way to our destruction; this is where we were headed. He stopped it.

"For thou hast delivered my soul from death, mine eyes from tears, and my feet from falling."

Psalm 116:8

Those that do not receive his free gift of righteousness and redemption will inevitably go to hell; this is where we were all headed. He will not force us to choose Him. The Father is gracious and has given us a free will. We are the ones that must choose. His hope is that we choose Him, choose life, and choose Jesus. God is not willing that any should perish but that all should come to repentance (2 Peter 3:9). His heart is that all would be saved. But all will not be; some will choose Jesus while others will hate Jesus.

"But thou hast in love to my soul delivered it from the pit of corruption: for thou has cast all my sins behind thy back."

Isaiah 38:17

Because He loved me, He was motivated to deliver me. He delivered my soul from the pit of corruption. I would have suffered in agony and terror were it not for my Savior and deliverer, for He has cast all my sins behind His back. He bore my grief and carried my sorrows. He was wounded for my transgressions and bruised for my iniquities. He took my load on His back. I was to carry it; it was mine. But He took it for me out of love.

"He delivereth and rescueth, and he worketh signs and wonders in heaven and in earth, who hath delivered Daniel from the power of the lions."

Daniel 6:27

The Lord is faithful to us. He is trustworthy and loyal, and we can put our utmost trust in Him. Heaven and earth will pass away, but His Word shall not pass away (Matthew 24:35). Even way back with Daniel and the lions' den, God was faithful; Daniel put his trust in God. He knew God would be with him. We must trust in God in His power to rescue us and deliver us. It is good to meditate on the miracles and wonders of God and to meditate on the works and miracles of Jesus in the gospels. We must imagine these wonderful things so that we can expect for signs and wonders to happen in our lives and through us. Jesus is the same today as He was yesterday and as He will always be.

"Then saith Jesus unto him, Get thee hence, Satan: for it is written, Thou shalt worship the Lord thy God, and him only shalt thou serve. Then the devil leaveth him, and, behold, angels came and ministered unto him."

Matthew 4:10–11

Jesus spoke to Satan. He spoke the Word. We cannot be passive or silent. The enemy will bring destruction if we are silent. Faith speaks. Jesus commanded him to leave; then He spoke the Word. If Jesus did this, we need to follow His example. This is the account of when Jesus fasted 40 days and 40 nights.

He was hungry, and the angels came to minister to Him. God met His need. Satan hates God's Word and doesn't want us to know its power and strength or its truth. We must get to know God's Word. We must meditate on it and know the truth of the Word deep in our hearts, so in times of need, we are ready to draw our sword, which is the Word of God, and pierce the darkness with its power.

"And, behold, there arose a great tempest in the sea, insomuch that the ship was covered with the waves: but he was asleep. And his disciples came to him, and awoke him, saying, Lord, save us: we perish. And he saith unto them, Why are ye fearful, O ye of little faith? Then he arose, and rebuked the winds and the sea; and there was a great calm."

Matthew 8:24–26

Jesus was not ruled by fear; He refused fear. He knew where it came from and what damage it could do if you opened your heart to it. He was led by the Spirit of God, by the Word of God, and by the peace of God. He knew His authority. He knew God was with Him. He was not ruled by circumstances. This was a great tempest that arose in the sea, enough so that the ship was covered with waves. That is pretty extreme, and yet Jesus was asleep. The disciples feared and were coming to Him to instigate fear in Him as well, but He would not have it. You either have faith or fear; if you have a lot of faith, you will have little or no fear. If you have a lot of fear, you may have little faith. Will we give in to fear or faith? He arose and took charge, for they would not. He rebukes the winds and the sea in His authority, and in the end, there was a great calm.

"And when he was come to the other side into the country of the Gadarenes, there met him two possessed with devils, coming out of the tombs, exceeding fierce, so that no man might pass by that way…So the devils besought him, saying, If thou cast us out, suffer us to go away into the herd of swine. And he said unto them, Go. And when they were come out, they went into the herd of swine: and behold, the whole herd of swine ran violently down a steep place into the sea, and perished in the waters."

Matthew 8:28,31–32

There is none that can stand up to the Lord of Lords and the King of Kings. Jesus is Lord, and He was not intimidated by any demon or any religious authority. Demons may have frightened the villagers away and showed themselves to be fierce, but they had to bow to Jesus. They were terrified of Him. They even asked if they could be allowed to go into the herd of pigs so that they could have a place to go. They need to have a body to be able to roam on this earth. He said, "Go," and they did. The whole herd of pigs ran violently down a steep hill into the sea and drowned in the water. We must keep our eyes on the one who is able to deliver, not the demons who deceive and have no authority. We stand behind the name, not in our own name. They are afraid of the name and His word. But they also know when a believer does not really know their authority in Christ.

"As they went out, behold, they brought to him a dumb man possessed with a devil. And when the devil was cast out, the dumb spake: and the multitude marveled, saying, It was never so seen in Israel."

Matthew 9:32–33

23

They brought to Jesus a man who was dumb and couldn't speak, for he was possessed with a demon that apparently caused the man not to speak. Jesus knew all things. He knew it was a demon. It doesn't say how long this man was possessed, but when Jesus cast the demon out, the man was able to speak. There was a multitude or a throng of people that wondered and marveled saying, "They had never seen this in Israel."

"Then was brought unto him one possessed with a devil, blind, and dumb: and he healed him, insomuch that the blind and dumb both spake and saw."

Matthew 12:22

This demon had caused the man to be blind and not to speak. There are times when demons attack the body in different ways, but we should never be afraid or be in terror of any demons, for they have been stripped and defeated. They have no power over us. Jesus has all power and has defeated the kingdom of darkness. Jesus healed this man, and he was free to see and free to speak. Praise God!

"And there was in their synagogue a man with an unclean spirit; and he cried out, saying, Let us alone; what have we to do with thee, thou Jesus of Nazareth? art thou come to destroy us? I know thee who thou art, Holy One of God. And Jesus rebuked him, saying, Hold thy peace, and come out of him. And when the unclean spirit had torn him, and cried with a loud voice, he came out of him."

Mark 1:23–26

This man was even in their synagogue, among them, with an unclean spirit. Maybe even several demons for they said, "Let us alone." They knew who He was—the holy one of God. We don't have to have conversations with demons, for they lie. Jesus told it to hold its peace, to be quiet. He said simply said, "Come out of him." Amplified says, "And the unclean spirit throwing the man into convulsions, and screeching with a loud voice, came out of him." The demon may have thrown a fit after Jesus commanded him to leave, but he did leave.

"And Jesus answering saith unto them, Have faith in God. For verily I say unto you, That whosoever shall say unto this mountain, Be thou removed, and be thou cast into the sea; and shall not doubt in his heart, but shall believe that those things which he saith shall come to pass; he shall have whatsoever he saith. Therefore I say unto you, What things soever ye desire, when ye pray, believe that ye receive them, and ye shall have them."

Mark 11:22–24

Jesus said, "Have faith in God." The Amplified explains this phrase as, "Have faith in God constantly." To have faith in God is to trust Him, to believe Him and what He says. Sometimes we fail because we are looking to ourselves. We think that we are not strong enough to believe or that we are unable to believe, but it is easy to believe that God can do anything. It is not supposed to be a struggle. Just decide to believe Him. Whosoever shall say to this mountain—what is your mountain? Throughout our lives, there will be many mountains for as long as we are in this world. You alone must speak to your mountain. Sometimes another believer can come alongside of you and pray for you, but you might as well learn to speak to the mountain as God intended you to.

Death and life are in the power of the tongue. This is how the kingdom of God operates. In the beginning, God said. Speak death to the mountain and life to your future. Envision it. Picture it in your heart. Remember, it's not according to your feelings.

"And he said unto them, Go ye into all the world, and preach the gospel to every creature. He that believeth and is baptized shall be saved; but he that believeth not shall be damned. And these signs shall follow them that believe; In my name shall they cast out devils; they shall speak with new tongues; They shall take up serpents; and if they drink any deadly thing, it shall not hurt them; they shall lay hands on the sick, and they shall recover. So then after the Lord had spoken unto them, he was received up into heaven, and sat on the right hand of God. And they went forth, and preached every where, the Lord working with them, and confirming the word with signs following. Amen."

Mark 16:15–20

These are some of the last instructions from Jesus to the disciples. In this instruction, the first word he uses is "Go." This is a verb, an action word. He is telling us what to do. We are the ones who will be doing it. He told us to go into all the world, to go and preach the gospel to everyone. The power of God is in the gospel (Romans 1:16). As you preach the gospel, signs will follow. The key is to believe. These signs will follow those that believe. We will be doing these works not in our own power but in the name of Jesus. These are not ordinary, everyday signs in the world. Most people don't go around casting out demons and speaking in new tongues. This is not the Old Testament—this is

New Testament living. And this was spoken after Jesus was raised from the dead. He spoke this just before he went to heaven to be with the Father. After He had spoken to them, he went to sit at the right hand of God. So they obeyed and preached everywhere. The Lord was in heaven, yes, but His Spirit was also living in them and working with them. They were not alone; He promised He would never leave them (Hebrews 13:5). He did as He promised. He confirmed His word with signs following.

"But Jesus beheld them, and said unto them, With men this is impossible; but with God all things are possible."

Matthew 19:26

Men are the creation from God. They are not God. Without His Spirit, we are nothing. With His Spirit, we have everything. We have His ability. Men, in themselves, are limited. They cannot accomplish what the almighty God can accomplish. Consider His majestic power. He is the creator of the crackling thunder and lightning. He made the breaking waves and the roar of the ocean deep. The clouds above all the earth were formed by Him alone, and He caused the rain to pour from the heavens. God alone made the lions that roam free and whales of the blue sea that frolic full of power. Who can tell the Almighty what to do? With God all things are possible!

"And he said unto them, I beheld Satan as lightning fall from heaven. Behold, I give unto you power to tread on serpents and scorpions, and over all the power of the enemy: and nothing shall by any means hurt you."

Luke 10:18–19

Jesus is the "I am." He was there when Satan fell as lightning from the heaven. He saw Satan stripped of his power and authority, not to mention all of his beauty. To fall means you are no longer in that place you were in. He fell because of pride. He was humbled by God, for he would not humble himself.

Jesus is the one with all authority. When He died on the cross, descended into hell, and rose again on the third day, He conquered Satan. He took the keys of hell and death and gave us authority. We have the power to tread on serpents and scorpions and over all the power of the enemy, and nothing shall by any means hurt you. You must use your faith and believe this in order to enjoy its benefits. His will is that you are protected. He thought of everything.

"For God so loved the world, that he gave his only begotten Son, that whosoever believeth in him should not perish, but have everlasting life."

John 3:16

God SO loved the world. There is no one that can ever say, "God doesn't love me." God's Word is truth and does not lie. This scripture states that He so loved the world. If you are on the earth today, that includes you. He proved His love by giving of his only Son. The scripture continues to say, "Whosoever." That also includes you, for each person, each human being, is a whosoever.

"Jesus answered and said unto her, Whosoever drinketh of this water shall thirst again: But whosoever drinketh of the water that I shall give him shall never thirst; but the water that I shall give him shall be in him a well of water springing up into everlasting life."

John 4:13–14

This can be spoken to any one of us. He is offering us a drink of the water that He gives us. It is not the same as the water we know, although you can look at the water that we are used to drinking as a parallel. We need water to live. We must have it to survive. But the issue with the physical water is that it needs to be replenished. Our thirst is quenched until we get thirsty again. With His Spirit living in us, we drink from the living waters. It is possible to be full, and stay full, as we let the Word of God dwell richly in us.

"I am the living bread which came down from heaven: if any man eat of this bread, he shall live for ever: and the bread that I will give is my flesh, which I will give for the life of the world."

John 6:51

Jesus came down from heaven. He calls himself the living bread, the Word. We are to eat this bread. The fleshly body needs bread to eat each day to sustain life. We need to eat of His word every day to sustain us, to grow, to be nourished and strengthened. As we accept Jesus and eat of Him, we shall live forever. Through His giving of His body, His life, the whole world is now able to have life because of Him. Without partaking of Him continually, you will have no life.

"It is the spirit that quickeneth; the flesh profiteth nothing: the words that I speak unto you, they are spirit, and they are life."

John 6:63

The Spirit brings life, and His words are Spirit, for they come from Him. Everything that comes from Him is life. When His spirit brings life to our spirit, it permeates through all of our being. His words are life to all of our flesh. They bring peace and life to our mind. The world puts great stock in having a perfect and beautiful outside body, but many do nothing on the inside. The kingdom of God starts from the inside out.

"The thief cometh not, but for to steal, and to kill, and to destroy; I am come that they might have life, and that they might have it more abundantly."

John 10:10

Why should we let Satan, who is the thief, steal from our lives any longer? As we dwell on the past and speak of the past, we are only helping him to dig our own grave. Why should we help him? He is the enemy, and he is defeated. Jesus came that we might have life and that we might have it more abundantly. The ones that come and receive and take it will be the ones who receive it.

"But ye shall receive power, after that the Holy Ghost is come upon you: and ye shall be witnesses unto me both in Jerusalem, and in all Judaea, and in Samaria, and unto the uttermost part of the earth."

Acts 1:8

Jesus didn't want to leave us alone. You can read more about the Holy Spirit in John 14. He is meant to be our helper and comforter, our advocate, and our teacher. He would not have given us the gift of the Holy Spirit unless we needed Him. With Him, we have the power of God to be witnesses throughout the earth. The Holy

Spirit also gives us boldness and power to have a more victorious Christian life. The Holy Ghost is a gift, and as you invite Him, He shall come upon you and you shall receive power from on high.

"And when the day of Pentecost was fully come, they were all with one accord in one place. And suddenly there came a sound from heaven as of a rushing mighty wind, and it filled all the house where they were sitting. And there appeared unto them cloven tongues like as of fire, and it sat upon each of them. And they were all filled with the Holy Ghost, and began to speak with other tongues, as the Spirit gave them utterance."

Acts 2:1–4

The disciples were all in unity, waiting. What was it like to hear this sound of a rushing mighty wind from heaven? Their hair and clothes must have been blowing as they sat waiting for this adventure. What an exciting experience God gave them. They were each amazed as they saw the lights of fire resting upon each of them. Every one of them were filled; Acts 1:15 says that there were 120 of them. When we receive the Holy Spirit, we have His power in us—the supernatural power of God. We were not meant to be ordinary. If the power of God that created the universe and raised Christ from the dead lives in you, how can you see yourself as only ordinary? We are His vessel; He moves through us, heals through us, and delivers through us. Tongues are a blessing that comes from God above. And God only gives good gifts.

"I am the door; by me if any man enter in, he shall be saved, and shall go in and out, and find pasture."

John 10:9

Always remember that Jesus is the door. He is the way, the truth, and the life. No man comes to the Father but by Him. He did the work; we receive the grace. It is not by our works, but by His works, His performance. Only He can save, and only He can give the rest that we need. Only He can provide the sweet freedom that we so desperately needed. All that is required is that we open the door and walk in. He did the work, and now He is waiting for you to respond. Walk and enter in the door of life, which is Jesus Christ, today.

About the Author

Linda Patarello is a born again Christian, and graduate from Charis Bible College in Colorado Springs, Colorado. She currently lives there, and spends most of her time spreading the truth about God's Love from the written Word. Linda is a California native with broad experience in leading praise & worship and songwriting. She believes that the highest calling is to worship the "Giver of All Gifts." She also believes we are born to pursue a relationship with God the Father, Jesus Christ and the Holy Spirit, and to share it with others. Her vision is to help people find true love for the Word of God, and to uncover its precious truths that are waiting to be revealed.

For More Information or to Contact the Author, Please Write to:

Linda Patarello
P.O. Box 7964
Colorado Springs, CO 80933

www.Heartsower.com

Prayer of Salvation

There is nothing more fulfilling in life than knowing that God loves you. God has made, and continues to make His love known to us by having sent His only begotten son, Jesus Christ, to die on the cross as payment for our sins and the injustices done unto us.

Has anyone willingly given up their life in exchange for yours, so that you may live? Jesus did. "Greater love hath no man than this, that a man lay down his life for his friends" (Jn. 15:13). Notice, that Jesus said this *before* he went to the cross. He laid down His life for us because he saw you and I, his friends, benefiting from this act of love.

You were the joy that was set before Jesus. "For the joy that was set before him [he] endured the cross, despising the shame, and is set down at the right hand of the throne of God" (Heb. 12:2). Only a true, selfless friend could love like this. Would you like to know the One Who finds you valuable, Who truly loves you? If you would like to ask Jesus to be your friend and your Lord and Savior, you can ask Him today. You can use your own words or pray,

"Lord Jesus, I want to know you, I want to be your friend. I invite you into my life, so that I may know you more. Be my saving friend, Lord and Savior. I am sorry for all my sins and past mistakes. Thank you for forgiving me and loving me, in spite of my past. You are my friend, even when I have no one else. I want to receive everything you have for me, even your Holy Spirit. Take control of my life, and through my relationship with you, let it grow and mature, and become a light unto others. Thank you for freeing me from sin and darkness, and for putting me in right-standing with you forever. I am saved! Thank you, Jesus! Amen!

If you prayed this prayer for the first time in your life, we believe that you are born again! Find a good Bible-based church, and connect with other believers. Please share your testimony or visit us online:

http://www.orionproductions.tv/contact-us.html

You can write to us:

Orion Productions

PO Box 51194
Colorado Springs, CO 80949

Blessings to you! From our staff at Orion Productions.

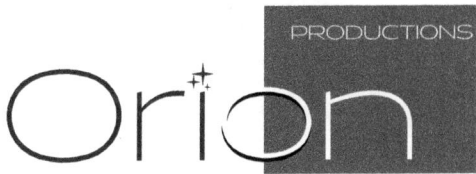

PRODUCTIONS

Orion

To make known the stories and accounts
of God's work in people's lives
through multimedia products and
services.

Our latest publishing information can be found
by visiting our website at:

www.orionproductions.tv/publishing.html